THE LIMITS OF SUR...

SIX DAYS ALONE!

Forest Survivor

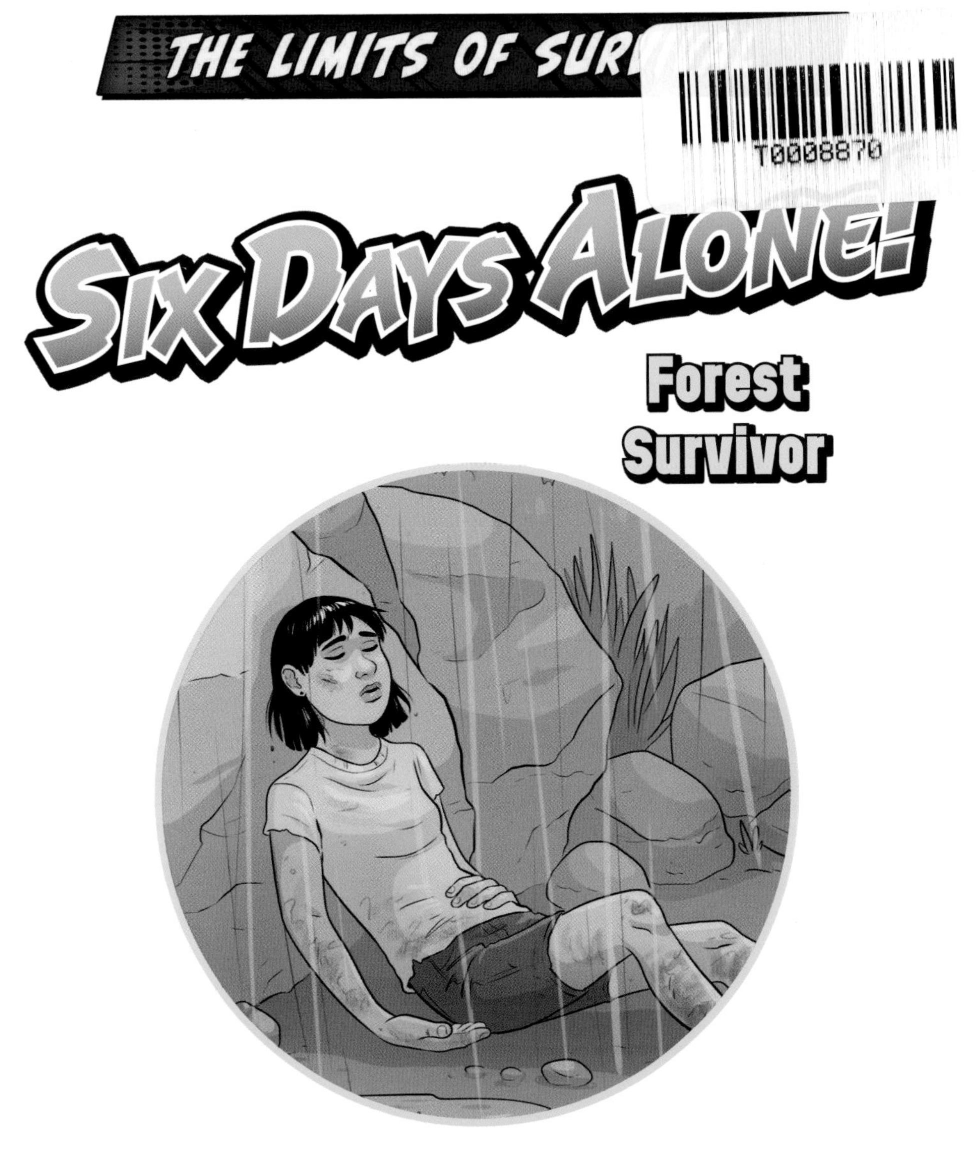

BY James Buckley Jr.

ILLUSTRATED BY Cassie Anderson

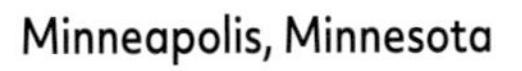
Minneapolis, Minnesota

Credits

Cover art by Cassie Anderson
Photos: 20 © Lorenzo18/Dreamstime.com; 21 © Helen Hotson/Dreamstime.com; 22 © Thomas Lindholm/Dreamstime.com; 23 © Carla Francesca Castagno.

Bearport Publishing Company Product Development Team
President: Jen Jenson; Director of Product Development: Spencer Brinker; Senior Editor: Allison Juda; Editor: Charly Haley; Associate Editor: Naomi Reich; Senior Designer: Colin O'Dea; Associate Designer: Elena Klinkner; Product Development Assistant: Anita Stasson

Produced by Shoreline Publishing Group LLC
Santa Barbara, California
Designer: Patty Kelley
Editorial Director: James Buckley Jr.

DISCLAIMER: This graphic story is a dramatization based on true events. It is intended to give the reader a sense of the narrative rather than a presentation of actual details as they occurred.

Library of Congress Cataloging-in-Publication Data is available at www.loc.gov or upon request from the publisher.

ISBN: 978-1-63691-992-8 (hardcover)
ISBN: 978-1-63691-999-7 (paperback)
ISBN: 979-8-88509-006-3 (ebook)

For more information, write to Bearport Publishing, 5357 Penn Avenue South, Minneapolis, MN 55419. Printed in the United States of America.

Contents

Chapter 1
A Hike Goes Wrong 4

Chapter 2
Lost and Alone 10

Chapter 3
Rescued! 16

Forest Survival Tips 20

Other Forest Survivors 22

Glossary 23

Index 24

Read More 24

Learn More Online 24

Chapter 1

A Hike Goes Wrong

A thick forest covers much of the area near Australia's east coast. In the midst of this wild land flows the Gorge Falls. Hikers often take a steep trail to see the beautiful waterfalls.

One of those hikers was Yang Chen, a student from China studying in Australia.
I'M EXCITED TO SEE THE FALLS!
THEY'RE BEAUTIFUL! AND IT SHOULD BE A PRETTY QUICK HIKE TO GET THERE.
Rain had made the trail more challenging than usual.

IT'S SO WET UP HERE! I'M GLAD I WORE MY BOOTS!
ALL THE RAIN HAS MADE THIS FOREST SO GREEN. BUT IT SURE MADE IT MUDDY, TOO!
I'M A LITTLE TIRED. CAN WE STOP AND REST?
WHY DON'T YOU TAKE A BREAK HERE. I'LL GO AHEAD AND MAKE SURE THE TRAIL IS OPEN.
THE FOREST IS JUST BEAUTIFUL. IT'S SO DIFFERENT FROM THE CITY WHERE I LIVE.

After her short rest, Yang was ready to catch up to her friend.
I SHOULD GET GOING.
I HOPE THIS IS THE RIGHT PATH...
HELLO? HELLO? IS ANYBODY THERE?
OH NO... WHERE'S THE TRAIL?!

Yang had no idea where she was. And she was all alone. What could she do?

Chapter 2
LOST AND ALONE
HELLO? HELLO?
I DON'T THINK MY CALL IS GOING THROUGH!
ARG! NOW THERE'S NO SIGNAL!
THE FOREST MUST BE TOO THICK HERE.
UGH! STILL NOTHING!
IT'S GETTING DARK... I NEED TO FIND SOME SHELTER FOR THE NIGHT. I CAN LOOK FOR HELP TOMORROW.

THIS BIG ROCK SHOULD KEEP THE RAIN OFF ME. I HOPE I CAN SLEEP!
SQUAWK
CLICK
CLICK
CRRRUNCH
SQUEAK
BZZZZ
Day Two
UGH! I DID NOT SLEEP WELL. I'M SO THIRSTY... AND HUNGRY. I GUESS I SHOULD GET MOVING.

I THINK I MIGHT HEAR SOMETHING AHEAD.
I HOPE IT'S SOMETHING TO EAT OR DRINK.
A STREAM! *HOORAY!* RUNNING WATER SHOULD BE SAFE TO DRINK.
AND WHAT'S THIS? HELLO, LITTLE GUY! OH, THIS CRAYFISH IS JUST TOO CUTE TO EAT.
BUT THERE MUST BE SOMETHING ELSE AROUND HERE... WHAT ABOUT THESE BERRIES?
ICK! THEY TASTE GROSS! THEY PROBABLY AREN'T SAFE.
MAYBE I SHOULD JUST WORK ON FINDING HELP.

OH NO, MY PHONE IS DEAD...
HELP! HELP! CAN ANYONE HEAR ME?
HELLO? HELP! CAN ANYONE— AAHH! A SNAKE!
WAIT, THIS SNAKE LOOKS PRETTY HARMLESS. I THINK I READ THAT ONLY THE COLORFUL ONES ARE DANGEROUS. WHEW!
Later, Yang heard a loud sound coming from the sky.
THUP THUP THUP
WHAT'S THAT?
A HELICOPTER! HEY! HEY! LOOK DOWN HERE! HEY!
THUP THUP
THUP
NO! THEY'RE FLYING THE WRONG WAY!
THUP THUP THUP

When Yang didn't return from her hike, **park rangers** set out to look for her. Some tried searching from a helicopter.
I DON'T SEE ANYTHING HERE!
LET'S FLY WEST. WE NEED TO KEEP LOOKING UNTIL WE FIND HER.
More park rangers gathered on the ground to search for Yang.

Some started looking at the spot where Yang had stopped to rest. They tried to find her trail.
YANG! MISS CHEN! CAN YOU HEAR US?
Other rangers used motorcycles to travel deeper into the forest.
Using an **inflatable** boat, some searchers followed the river that led to the falls.
The day turned rainy.
And there was still no sign of Yang.

Chapter 3

Rescued!

Day Six
Meanwhile, the search continued.
SEE IF YOU CAN CLIMB THAT CLIFF TO LOOK UP THERE.
THIS WON'T BE EASY.
I KNOW, BUT WE HAVE TO TRY. SHE COULD BE ANYWHERE.
WAIT... DID YOU HEAR SOMETHING?
YES. IS THAT ANOTHER SEARCH TEAM CALLING OUT?
HELP! UP HERE! CAN YOU SEE ME?
IT'S YANG!
WE SEE YOU! STAY THERE! DON'T TRY TO CLIMB DOWN!
WE FOUND HER! WE FOUND HER!

THANK GOODNESS I HEARD THEM TALKING.
I'M SAVED... I CAN'T BELIEVE IT!
ARE YOU HERE TO RESCUE ME?
YES, WE'VE GOT YOU, MISS CHEN. YOU'RE SAFE NOW.
LET'S GET YOU SOME WATER—AND I THINK YOU'LL NEED DRY SOCKS!
SHE'S ALIVE! WE'RE BRINGING HER DOWN NOW.
DON'T WORRY, WE'VE GOT YOU!

MISS CHEN? ARE YOU ALL RIGHT?
YES, I'M OKAY. THANK YOU FOR FINDING ME!
WE CAN'T BELIEVE YOU SURVIVED OUT THERE FOR SIX DAYS!
Later, at the hospital...
...AND I SAW A LARGE BROWN SNAKE THAT I THOUGHT WAS SAFE.
SAFE? THAT COULD HAVE BEEN A BROWN TAIPAN— ONE OF THE DEADLIEST SNAKES IN THE WORLD!
WELL, SNAKES OR NO SNAKES, I'M LUCKY TO BE ALIVE.

Forest Survival Tips

If you plan to visit a forest, follow these tips to help you survive.

- Before you go, study a map of the area. Plan **routes** to the places you want to visit.
- Tell people where you will be going and when you plan to return.
- Bring a cell phone with a full charge, but be aware that **remote** areas of the forest may not have cell phone service.
- Pack the clothing you will need to stay warm or cool, depending on what the weather will be like.

- Bring a compass to help you know which direction you are going.
- Bring extra food and water, as well as a small first aid kit, just in case you get lost.
- Have brightly colored clothing to put on so a search team can spot you more easily if you get lost.
- Bring matches and lighters to start a fire to stay warm.
- Bring a whistle to help you get attention from others if you are lost.
- Build or find a shelter for protection from rain, wind, and snow.

Other Forest Survivors

Gene Penaflor became separated from his friends while hunting in the woods. To make matters worse, he fell and was knocked out. When he woke up and realized he was lost, Gene set up a camp. He built a fire to stay warm. Gene looked for wild berries and small animals to eat. At one point, Gene heard helicopters searching for him, but he couldn't get their attention through the thick trees. He was finally found, weak but alive, after 19 days alone in the forest.

Sisters Aubrey and Grace got lost after the sun went down while they were walking through the woods. The girls were alone and afraid, but they did what they could to be found. Aubrey finally got a signal on her cell phone and called for help. Grace hit her light-up sneakers with the hope that someone would notice the bright lights. Eventually, **expert** rescuers used **infrared equipment** that helped them see in the dark. The girls were found and returned home safely.

GLOSSARY

expert someone who knows a lot about something or can do something really well

inflatable something that can be filled with air to float

infrared equipment devices that can improve vision in the dark by making warm objects stand out

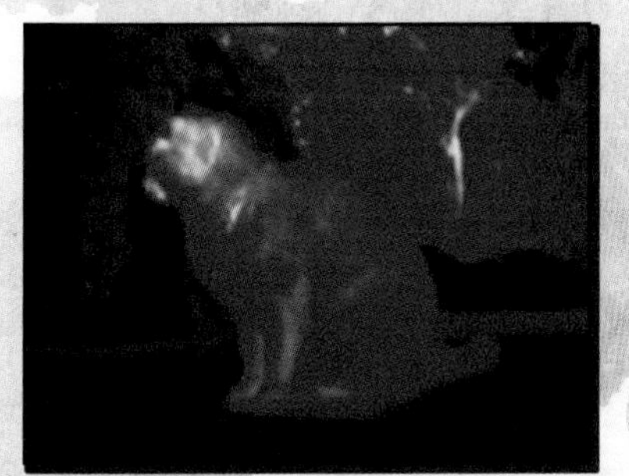

park rangers people trained to help others in large parks and nature areas

remote very far away from where other people are

routes paths between places

shelter a safe place that covers or protects people or animals

signal the electronic connection between cell phones

Index

Australia 4–5
brown taipan 19
cliff 17
crayfish 12
Gorge Falls 4
helicopter 13–14, 22
inflatable boat 15
motorcycles 15
park rangers 14–15
Penaflor, Gene 22
snake 13, 19
survival tips 20–21
trail 4–7, 15

Hudak, Heather C. *Rainforest Survival Guide (Brave the Biome)*. New York: Crabtree Publishing, 2021.

Jaycox, Jaclyn. *This or That? Questions about the Wilderness (This or That? Survival Edition)*. North Mankato, MN: Capstone Press, 2022.

Kingston, Seth. *Hiking (Wilderness Adventures)*. New York: PowerKids Press, 2021.

Learn More Online

1. Go to **www.factsurfer.com** or scan the QR code below.
2. Enter **"Six Days Alone"** into the search box.
3. Click on the cover of this book to see a list of websites.